THE ALL-PURPOSE MAGICAL TENT

DATE DUE

NOV 2 9 2010		
FEB 17 2011		

DEC 0 8 2009

THE
ALL-PURPOSE
MAGICAL
TENT

LYTTON
SMITH

NIGHTBOAT BOOKS
NEW YORK

Cover image: "At the Vermont State Fair, Rutland"
Kodachrome photograph by Jack Delano, September 1941
Courtesy of Library of Congress, Prints & Photographs Division

Design and typesetting: LaSalle Enterpress
Text set in Perpetua

Library of Congress Cataloging-in-Publication Date

  Smith, Lytton, 1982-
  The all-purpose magical tent: poems / Lytton Smith.
  p. cm.
  ISBN 978-0-9767185-0-5 (alk. paper)
  I. Title.
  PS3619.M5917A78 2009
  811'.6--dc22
  2008050852

Nightboat Books
New York
www.nightboat.org

For my family:

Heather, Brian, Warwick, Garth,
without whom none of this.

Jess, pondering mind, fellow traveller,
in shelter, in island & affiliation.

Contents

Foreword by Terrance Hayes

In his essay "The Novel as Spectacle" Italo Calvino says writing "like the making of spectacle [takes] place as it were before the reader's eyes in a kind of dialogue with [the writer's] reactions of curiosity, fear, laughter or tears." His definition of spectacle (which might also be another word for magic) suits the wonder of these poems. In *The All-Purpose Magical Tent* we are witness to a broad, slanted imagination which manifests itself not only in inexplicable subjects (a manual for weather, interior horticulture, motorists' gloves and leathers!), but in the drunken diction of Lytton Smith's sentences: "Edge of the furze I've hidden and there is goose / want, birdfright." Whoa... Some poets labor for years—or record the music of aviaries and asylums—in search of a syntax this particular, this peculiar. Some poets dream of inventing and reinventing the kinds of forms we find here: the off-rhyme of the terza rima, "Annuls the Space/Time Experience"; the deft sestina "Animals and Vehicles / Vehicles and Animals"; the atmospheric prose sequence, "If You Could See the Motorists' Gloves and Leathers!"; the mock essay, "Manufacturing Culture." Every line is delivered with a perversity that bewilders and delights.

Ultimately, I love this collection for its crafty displacements. As the opening line of the sequence "Monster Theory" suggests ("It is always at the outset a displacement—"), we are asked to both submit and assent to Smith's shifting, near imaginary landscapes and scenarios. The poems both enact and address a world that will "drop away about you." They present the "[f]ear of ground opening / to absence like the magician's trick cabinet." And just as Calvino would have it, the poet's reactions of curiosity, fear, laughter, or tears are ours. This writer's sheer audacity becomes not only a spectacle but a sensibility.

The late Frank Stanford, another poet of visionary intensity and bedeviled diction, once said, "Poetry sometimes is like going along in a big rig with no one else on the roads...only the sound of your own voice trying to get in touch." For bystanders watching this rig go by, it is a dizzying experience—the sort that bobbles and opens the head. This poetry inhabits a world of its own—equally foreign and distinct, dazed and acute. This poet has a warning for those of us entering his tent of enchantment: "Leave your instruments / at the entrance. We live between weather / and earthlight: there is no use for them here...." Beware, be struck, be open to it.

Terrance Hayes, June 2008

Generation followed generation. They forgot many things, they devised many things. Their tradition of the greater world they came from became mythical in colour and uncertain.

—H. G. Wells

Manual for Weather

All that is left of weather
is how it is written. A deepening as it builds
does not tension the calves; boulder winds

arrive without the warning of hook or bow
echo, without change to the anemometer.
What we know of wind shift and lapse rate

is hazarded. Among the civil twilight
of these caverns we wait out occluded fronts,
believe lake effect conditions and also warmer

prevailing. There is rain shadow and undercast
in every recess and no device for fathoming
tule fog or advection. Our advance signal

the small crafts which trial how fetch
strengthens plough wind into straight-line.
From shore we see them blown towards

us overtaken by storm and what it brings.
Our panic to shelter the thin herds, to gather
our frail homes before the backscatter.

It is said there are clouds where sight
does not reach—comma, anvil, torn—
between horizon and ceiling. Our technicians

take soundings, map our annual weather
patterns and hint to forecast; an earlier time
would have favoured them for soothsayers.

Welcome, friend. Leave your instruments
at the entrance. We live between weather
and earthlight: there is no use for them

here, no music without weather. Silence,
words folding into it, enough.

Scarecrow Work

Bury your eyes in late barley. Your congregation
sleeps in the baptismal river—an answer to thirst,
     a satisfaction—a flock

that would not shepherd. When told the abandoned
do not companion despair they still sought flight,
     sought turning from water.

Their restlessness a dusk leave of settlement; yours
a crowsighted knowledge: how you were chosen
     for laying on hands,

how your congregation rests riverbed for your mercy
is unbound. Your lesson: what will not scatter is safe,
     is dove, is olive return.

Hereafter

This world will drop away
about you. At its return

you know no longer
the insignia of hereafter

as you stand at the same
meeting of streets you did.

Could touch have done this?
Wish to be given this time

over but slow (think sundial
not stopwatch) but not

for remember: this world
can no longer be termed:

for artifice, replace edifice;
for secret, draught of record

hubstoned; or understand
embrace as what monuments.

Wish for this time given
over you won't remember

bricks dissembling about you
or scaffold ouster. Touch

is all is given you and haste
governs the constructed.

The Lost Tin Myth

You come ashore to sight of castings,
an engine house, far-off silhouettes

of fieldwork, minehaul. The sound
of this island is assembly, manufacture

knolled into landscape. You breathe
in air and taste ore. If you expected

welcome, you were mistaken.
What you know of this place—hills

the beaten texture of worked metal,
a winter the white silver of tin

won from cassiterite—are the elements
of something approaching myth.

The trick by which an island disappears
is not through a trapdoor in a metaphor

of the cardboard theatre of the world,
is not the shift of tectonic plates:

the island becomes the tale of island;
its inhabitants, figures of inhabitants.

Morning Is Light Coming and Geography

Nerves taut. Nerves taught. I can't curtail
the wood as it draws closer, this advance of foliage.

I'm watching the natural world turned human agent.
Distance collapsing as though the theatrical might

not be staged. As though a stage for the meeting
of war, doorstep, and on-going is the wood as it closens

disquiets the horses and outward walls. I wish
my armour ornamental. Not itself the body's cage

but the body's form. The horses' sweat is mine
their paw and scream is, I'm stabled here, inert

as precipice. My physicians say the spirits of animals
flow within our hollow nerves. Armour me, humour me,

this one last fervour. Favour. Night falls to cover over
our loss or light survival. Fails.

                              I think of them the same.

Seven Movements from the
Repertoire of the Unnamed

I

These fingers. They're nimble
and won't be stilled.

II

It gladdens me to have playthings
littler than me. I wish they'd grow,
though. I break into them too quickly.
It is too difficult to see what in them spins.

III

How far a spider	can string a net
I pass the moons	in study—fierce
in concentration—	at how secrets
cannot be kept—	spool always out.

IV

It falls out that seduction sits not well with me.

V

These fingers. You'll never guess
    but my mind is sharp
    and taken with riddles.

VI

Do you come out at night
the way I do because the light hidden
in this web of darkness strings us along?

The castle does it too, though you're
too little to see that. Belittling,
it is. A bright coax trills me to the tower,
until my cheek is flesh to flesh with stone.
But I'm not yet wished for.

VII

I'll break you, I know. I always do.
These fingers must have a thing to tend to.
They're nimble. I do not mean to.

Interior Horticulture Affair

Belief would be an orchard
among furniture (but uneasy:
bookshelfs, cedar). Did think
greenfingered and invested

tablets, appropriate peat, some
whisper. Shoots, but doubt:
climate; how sapling the trunks;
budworms. This dwarf orchard

I have failed. Uproot, removal.
This diseased. This of seedless
stock. Am left with cuttings,

with planters empty, armchair,
with thoughtful of autumn,
with trellis-and-vine intention.

Charm Against the Loss of Crops

Wheat ear wheat chaff fallow
wheat ear wheat chaff
fallow, wait out   the time
                          until we can unseal our stone
                    reliquary of seed and learn again to coax

with warmth a thing organic
and vital. We advanced
by erasures   pausing only
                          to hide the germ of an idea
                    as deep and frozen as imagination allowed

hoping the mountain storehouse
would change nothing
but suspend   the whittling
                          of our regions to arid
                    and monotone. If seeds remember growth

after centuries and can shape
leaf petal and stamen
when sown   in earth
                          reclaimed, we will know
                    living persists, recovered from a lost past

[. . .]

The Tightrope Walker's Childhood

Fear of wheatfields. Fear of groundbeetles.
Fear of where the tree trunk disappears

below ground. Fear of ground opening
to absence like the magician's trick cabinet.

She can sleep only on water and fitfully.
Footfall is an act of brevity then she is

soundlessly at your shoulder. From stilts,
rooftops, belltowers she studies faraway,

learns to think as a wing-walker, to harness
bird's-eye view: rivers are blue scarves,

an oxbow lake fits in the small of her back,
fields are a patchwork she can fold

about her at night. Here, afloat above
a sawdust ring, the audience's faces

safe as farms distance has made small, rope
is all the faith she needs. This is no feat

of balance. This is belief and aversion,
this is how earth becomes afterthought.

Earliest Known Record of a Carousel Device

Curtainfall, and the familiar conjuring of canvas
out of tents. This itinerance, this merry going round

from town to town a strange and laboured way
to move about the country. We're at our usual tricks:

carousel dismantled, the wanton clowns lounge
noselessly among tent pegs and the inseparable

trapeze artists stretch out on the elephant's back.
Our topped-and-tailed master journeys a map

with his white-gloved finger, teases from the legend
where next we'll peddle our circular display,

and here I am, a tired tamer of lions coiling rope
into departure. Whenever anyone talks of ends

to such uprooting, of setting down, a hush settles
on the shoulders, there's a sudden need to tether

ourselves to half-paced rehearsals, to bury a head
between the lion's teeth. At night someone's disappeared.

As our patched cavalcade meddles its roundabout route
to a greener village green, I watch landscape unroll

a sequence of repeated trees, electricity pylons
strung along, ridges sloping past. The edge

of the contemporary gone before I can mean it.

If You Could See the Motorists'
Gloves and Leathers!

Tonight, there's a lot of fancy cars in the All-Purpose Magical Tent. Fordcedes, Lamboursches. How they gleam. The sheen on them's been shun so shiny they would dazzle you, Leif Erikson, if only you had eyes for it. This time been spent on buff and burnish and what yield of decals you'd not believe. Some pass this way rumouring electric windows and yes there's skeptics and yes there's those who'll have you unfond of such manipulation but these are tonight the fancy cars— turn about the rows and ranks with me, the while they've been here's not lost their lustre, these sedans, saloons, these limouscenes. Until the dandies come back swagger and with girl they're ours, we're up to the inflated headlamps in them. Yes, here and there of cracks, but did you see such license ever, of plates yellow also? Why look to jolly along, Francis Younghusband? There's time for dawdle yet in the marvellous tent, saving your umbrella for an afterwards unfurling.

If You Could See the Motorists'
Gloves and Leathers!

Ever throw the discus?
For there's such a thing as a wheel Neanderthal but it was us
who capped the hubs and there's one lying there. And get me
started on upholstery, the blustered leather of these ought-to-
mobiles. If you'd eyes for it you'd not see the rips or padding
shedded out but instead the finery, the almost-frippery, the
splendid elementary fabrics—yes, John from Mandeville,
you're within the fantastical tent, these are the fancy cars, and
they're meant for habitat. Years back you'd hear gents with
floozies floundering in from the fairground gulled by the hot
air of zeppelins and the balderdash of sky and could you see
them now their brains and hearts taken with what shuttles
space about. All this up aboveness! I'm a man of tread and
chassis and not for ferrous wheels, even when the dans who
drove here felt their tires tire out and jacked with bricks the
axles. The odd door's missing, there's nesting in some trunks,
and I've heard the word *decrepit* bandied but within this canvas
there's a lot of fancy cars tonight.

Structural for the Tent

Mainstay. Ringside. Acts. The audience is meant

To believe in the tent even when they pass on

And it's dismantled—apparition. "The night sky

Was in there. The full moon. The clowns wore

The gravediggers' smiles." Circular and itself

In a field. The events transpiring within an illusion

The performers and watchers aspire to maintain.

"The lions I think Africa. The trapeze intercontinental.

We were magicked away." But there's nothing magical

About the magical. The audience invents a moment

The disappeared reappear. Any moment now. Now.

Now. I've watched the sleight-of-hand from the gods

And found it wanting—each act I can't take back.

If You Could See the Motorists'
Gloves and Leathers!

Secret, Sir Henry Stanley: I'd never seen one. Rusted as I am I
must've had a boyhood, boyish but in my looking the cars had
haunches, mouth to cud and sweat their flanks. There's folk'll
never leave the fairground, root to it and hard to believe
they've feet to keep the floor. The transfixed horses of the
carry/sell had me. We rode, our goldfish in individual oceans,
and I earned my dimes at barter. You see me uniformed with
pockets deeply nickelled for a Thundervette. Another round of
jaunters gollying through I'll have my saving, Amelia Earhart.
An oxide but colours them must be of late not the way a gloom
nests in on us. Yes I thirst but one's coming who'll bring a
cloudy lemonade. What takes my mind off is spit polish these
hoods. To what end, Saint Francis Xavier? As if there's other
purposes we're willed for, Saint Francis Xavier!

In the Last Days of the Circus

Months after the human cannonball was buried
in his cannon the ringmaster kept to his trailer.
The last of the circus folk passed their hours

keeping blades from the strongman, playing
to dwindling in a town where the sun
did not rise so much as leach colour to the sky

until you knew you'd missed dawn. Rigging again
the big top came apart in their hands, newest victim
to the rubber man's cabinet of exotic moths,

and the ringmaster emerged on cue, hands gloved
in white silk. The circus folk assembled, the fat lady
with hipbones protruding, the fire-eater wearing

a neck brace, the silent troupe of monkeys.
The three aging giants each in an olive jacket.
The townsfolk watched them kneel in the mud

as the other acts clambered on their shoulders,
on each other's shoulders, as the giants unfolded
at the joints, creaking in the wind. From within

the impromptu pyramid the ringmaster was heard
So this is what it means to see further and beyond
as the structure buckled about him and was gone.

[. . .]

The Anvil That Comes Before Your Civilisation

At pause from our forging
there's water, tern and gull

disappearance. To ocean
our wanderers surrender

on crafts of shaped wood;
to ocean we surrender

treasured heroes on ships
lit with a fire we're learning

the wielding of: a fox chars,
a limb does not recover.

In fire the glint in earth
found with heron-eyes

softens slag to the kiln.
We've poor altars for metal.

We temper copper on the back
of toppled menhirs, stone

columns with small brunt
for the harrying blow.

Land from the ocean
is rare spectacle, kindling

tales of the bidding horizon;
then we again to our smelt,

to the infirm anvil and what
weirds such forge and forage.

Tales of the Northern Settlement

Told by a Widow

Beyond chalk-white bears: tradition.
Alone, I weave clothes for the settlement,
softening the fur with my teeth, binding

the hollow hairs of winter animals into skins.
Disappeared in them, children sealbark
wolfhowl and otter about the huts;

at times men don't return from the hunt.
The rest bring speared animals whose eyes
look strange. Lately, they refuse the kill

and instead sculpt antic gargoyles who stare
from our domed houses. Out past the bears
not meant to shape such memorial.

Told by a Child

In the driftwood we find unfamiliar dead fish,
transparent and hardened, and in their mouths
thin white skins speckled black

and with frozen images of a place
where the land has always been swamped
or left parched. I long to tell its spirits

we, too, are without ceremony, only the motions our daily
chores have: building and taking apart, the tide.

But in this vastness we're not allowed.
On unsteady feet we rescue flotsam—
without us no flooded gimbal

to pass from hand to hand. One winter
a forest washes ashore; the caught acorns
leaden our pockets but we let them there

to see when at our fingers' ends they'll mulch,
and in this forest we look solemnly
for gods and know weapons were shaped

in such a place. As we grow older, we leave
coast and venture inland. A rope loosed
into fissure hits bottom; our stagger

pitches us toward silent tunnels knowing
what we earth up we'll have to cast back.
We stray farther than any before us.

Told by a Wife

The day he returned, apart from the others,
shucked his blood-matted furs and sealed himself
in our hut, I did not know what silver was,

the use of exchange. We threw voices
at the lone chink in the hut's walls,
and it shuttled back blunt gutturals.

Skinless, there's little time, then the body ceases.
Mutiny in the lungs. The chest struggles
for drawings-in of air, forbidding speech.

Fingers fail; the mind delirious increasingly.
Before his end, he wrote of a civilisation
found beneath stone in unfathomable chaos.

(No words of what shame he owned.)
When he was gone, his brothers concealed
themselves under wooden boats, and at night

the water scuttled them, set them loose.
We watched the horizon for their return
and soon forgot they had ever been here.

Before long we forgot white could mean
surrender, and when men appeared
from the sea we lacked clement gestures,

wheeling our arms to no end. Someone
launched a white orb into the air, war
began, the children nowhere to be found.

There Was No Winter In It

Edge of the furze I've hidden and there is goose
want, birdfright. Pond bank, stagnation, but smell
in the nostrils reminds—*damp, leaf*—colludes
nerves. Twitch among this still, will I quarrel
dirt and give away? Crime mine, shame, or soon
if not. Watched arc and course of what departs
heights and thought, *Birthright this familiar coop
of perpetual woodland.* But here is tar
hardening and unwooding for the heather.

Smell, damp. Here among the panicked quiet
of birds with dark, of undisturbed water,
hide beyond ground? I'll limb trees, not be caught
nor to earth but air. Imagine escape
love without feathers, hereditary trait.

Monster Theory

I

It is always at the outset a displacement—
[the monster] is fragment, obscured glance,
suspicion, boneshard, is one town over
and can be seen footprint or silhouette
at the Gates of Difference, dependent
on their unlocking. It does not test
the height of the wall, try to scale it;
is bound to rules even in deformity.

II

All cartographers are men and all their wives,
all their thimble & needle wives, could not understand
the sense of scale such men are born into:

how borders fit within the boundaries of a singlesheet,
how men are meant to region the diminished globe,
mark its latitudes. At the centre of the map they place

their town. Concentric from it, the foreign. The island
of only-women. The creatures with heads for stomachs.
[The monster] finely etched. Re-drawn. Drawing closer.

III

An imagination of cartographers
A fumbling of daughters   An aloneness of [monsters]
A warmongering of sons
A body of woodsmen   A liminality of [monsters]

A confusion of daughters   An expectance of hermits
A body of townswomen
A luminosity of torchbearers An affection of hermits

A deconstruction of record-keepers
A secondsight of burghers
A *hic est monstrum* of [monsters] A faraway of [monsters]
A one town over of [monsters]

IV

Thumbscrew: would not compass thumb.

Iron maiden: the points bent on contact.

Cauldron of boiling water: stench, but not of burning flesh.

Buried alive: restored, [the monster] emerges from a grave.

Torn apart by horses: horses expired.

Steel chamber: [the monster] could not have escaped
      more quickly.

Drowning: the haul dwindles; of the occasional trawler, no news.

*Gaol cell. Handcuff. Bullet (silver). Banishment. Pleading. Offer of
      Surplus and Fealty:* ineffectual.

Rendering as Myth: [the monster] never seen twice
      in the same form.

V

The cartographer remembers the anniversary
of his daughter's disappearance, redrawing
the map he made for her earliest birthday:

the town, its alleyways, and beyond the limits,
slant-script as she asked him, *Here Be Monsters.*
He colours it with petals picked and crushed

for dye in the nearby wood. He uses sapling
branches for its frame, gathered searching
where she must now be. Hanging it outside

for rain to loosen it, he mouths the old warning:
inter [the monster's] corpse at a fork in the road
that when it escapes from the grave it will not

know the path to follow. His sleep is interrupted
by the open and crash of shutter on window:
his daughter taken, the town woken in light.

VI

"Inter my corpse where two roads converge
at the gallows: the monster always escapes
& I must not know which road leads to you."
"..

....

...."
"The monster exists as harbinger to crisis,
devil's advocate to the identity. I do not call
these limbs misshapen & yet my horns ruin
how you category." "...........................

.............................." "So be it. I am
lodging-house keeper to terror, I am host
to dis-ease. I consent." "........................

...................." "In time, their summons:
come tempt, come captivate, come as what
we are not & how we will rise against you.
So it is I police the borders of the possible,
serve to remind how fearful exception is."
"..

...."
"You of all should know fear of the monster
is a kind of desire, a way of loving without
the difficulty of touch." "......................

....

......................." "If your hands grant
a life I could not have imagined, the amber
of electric through the body, I have seen

also your weeping after." "....................
....
....
........." "No. Your presence threatens a chaos
beyond my means: when I allowed you here,
trusted to you quill & the mark of my skin-"
"..............." "I was mistaken. Monster's role
is to reveal; if monster becomes progenitor,
what then?" "..........." "I am made uncertain
by you-" "......................................
....
...."

"They will arrive to find me & you tearful.
It does not matter you are unharmed.
One of their youth must kill me, his wounds
not mortal but legendary. He must become
hero & I allowed to go. Inter me as I asked.
My survival is to emerge from a grave, await
summons. You to the hero's bedchamber; I
to brief solitude. There is some peace in life.
I remember you." "............................
....
...."

Kingdom of the Blind

You court blindfold,
cloth across the closed eye

and here
in the village

a man who has twice looked
at eclipse   lived for the telling

&

If hindsight were clearer charted
you would have found him as he sat
by the one road into the settlement
anxious for the hornbeam sound
of carriage wheels

You wait instead
for the scent and taste of the man

(you will know him ash and singe and know him fired clay)

&

Taste is a parched unbudding
you learn
demur, silence, the feel gaze has

[...]

"[...] language as an unhomely dwelling place"

Rust on the sickles, cliffs discoloured, the arterial
road approaching the unexplained monument

    I think of you. Parallel this westering narrative

I'll offer the village station. We'll share places I hope
sidings are mossed. We'll share their sound—

    glance, accomplice, the still of tiger lilies orange

and unrepentant in fall—call it the remnant porch
of the abandoned house, the lights of the north.

    These are scenes I'll ask you tell again,

the comfort in the company of footfall. A lapse
of residence we'll set to horse. My eye follows

    where your hand suggests direction is language

unhomely in the contours of a manuscript. A clearing
and its boundary. The hybrid wildlife of irises visible

    in the foliage. Language, we are moving on again.

The Wide Receiver Declares Himself Ready

"Go long," you say, "get open," though you mean
Why don't you tie your sorrows to your saddle-bow

and ride singing forth?—and I set off, gone beyond
the last bus-stop, its shelter idling, I continue

past the moon landing staged in a barn
the government has blacked-out and starred

with phosphor. I keep going, past the last whalers,
sea-town inns, verge-of-the-afterlife churches

clergied by sailors the ocean spewed back, I reach
the harbour where townsmen jettison the cargo

of tea leaves, I travel waters where the Armada lies
foundered from cannon-breach, I pass Chaucer's company

returning, their contest forgotten as the inn approaches,
I go beyond the fifteen-foot walls of the Tower of London

to the battle at Hastings where the Normans feint flight
then charge then rout, and here, "Go long, get open," means

"stand firm," means "to the death," and when I call "let fly"
you do, arrow or pigskin lost in the sun and I'm waiting

and waiting and you won't believe the far I've gone.

Annuls the Space/Time Experience

And Kate is gone—some climate tension—flown
the kind of coop we thought we'd built hereto
and how the world's less blond than once, and no,

no key's been left for locking the lean-to
so vagrant's grown the inners, kind of nest
we called a bird's hereto, with moss ado

about the walls, their lichen grey, then next
the barn then next the miniature hamlet
so what's to do but build our balsa wrecks

of ships from kits (no point in paint, forget
ideas of paint, of colour), let the rest
unravel Jacob's ladder-like and let

achromatic roses, coals, red-lettrist
days be the days we think of Trevor, where
we left him teaching plastic soldiers whist

and gin in suits of cards too similar, war
of spade on spade. That's where this leaves more than
us. Science has machines for finding lairs

behind the mazes of fancy French *jardins'*
obscure designs, though the -ometer's cracked gauge
or would-we-call-it face reveals less than

predicted once, since Prudence sailed the Cape
of Charm. Is this the dream of language,
a trap with rusted hasp (suggests escape

but offers teeth) the way we shear the hedge,
hedge our bets and better yet the tethered way
we set our teeth to task? The string that led

toward the centre became knotted, frayed
hindrance of minotaurs, where Ben has left
a written note as if to say the lair

is love of lair, the lyre a stringed bereft
of am, the lure just that, another dream
of language heard as fluid as adrift

within this sea of goings from the scene
we thought we'd held to, here. But isn't to hold
the thing, and not the thing that's held? The feel

of having found ourselves paused in the field
of water caught in the fountain, and slipped
to patterns? Logic won't let us withhold,

we'd take up welding could we, learn the ship
of draughtsmen or the work of thieves, we'd have
ourselves the skills of craftsmen widely, flinch

the candlesticks but end the same way, trapped
in the mantrap and left to think from sense
to sound, to loiter out the time and grab

what's tragic, goat: we've fallen for our absents
and this is then the dream of language,
of those who've left, and left us with their absence.

Manufacturing Culture

In this context, apparently trivial issues such as whether students should be taught to draw the human figure assumed a tremendous symbolic significance. No longer did pivot-boned apprentices steeped in the deep brown light of late afternoon labour over musculature and flexed tendon. Officials wearing nosegays of loosestrife and in robes of purpure received investiture; epistled polemics were delivered by citizens familiar to pulpits. Others improvised lecterns. Medical students avoided conversations of the skeleton, fearing misconstruction. Textbooks were found, burned, and rose from the ashes devoid of the illustrated human anatomy. Clerks with whiteout gumshoed the streets, erasing from pictures both within and external to civic buildings the semblances of men. The zealous took exception to the simian, raiding apiaries and zoos where vigilant keepers averred their orangutans to be malnourished North American Bears. A New Age of Kidnappings began, cults of disappearance, such fervour there was to avoid imitation of the body. Former artists' models ill-fitted with clothes stupored in gutters; caryatids absented themselves from public display; gargoyles waited frantically to see what of this would be brought against them. Cousins, in-laws, in one case a boy of seven informed on loved ones who had not surrendered calipers, rasps, chisels, or easels. The Great Masters declaimed against this and yet their landscapes became thin in multitude; that year's National Exhibition featured works set only in abandoned hamlets. Market-tenders reported a revival in profit margins of fruits domestic and exotic. Coming upon the stalls, tourists reacted with surprise (the pictures in the guide had been of unattended alleys of produce). From underneath the city, revolutionaries championed the inalienable right to gestural depiction, freedom to the study of such. This movement was without legs and was overcome by a proliferation of official histories depicting the student-artist with jaundiced cheeks, eyes sunk to caldera. The Council was at times waylaid by an upstart member of the Opposition who questioned the turn of events; always the Council's reply affirmed Schools of Design should teach only skills strictly necessary to the ornamental.

Circus Memory

The bearded lady

       cries into a torn playbill
          the flat marquee

lying   ground like   moon
   no   pulled from   lake.
    ,   strains   the clowns' tune
        .   wake

proceeds: motley
            ringmaster
  lies   lion's cage,
      . Once, she asked

          he'd   leave.
He stared at her,   ,
       to the sky,   his heels,
      her,   ,

       asked, *Where?*

News of the Ornithologists

A colleague lasted out the war among a siege
    of ground hornbills;

more emerge from hide-nests of gull and merlin,
    a loomery of guillemots.

From carmine bee-eaters I learned painted wing,
    a thirst for insects.

We observed how birds mob about a settled place
    when intruded on:

they have their perennial scree while we, pigeon-toed,
    trace ways back

to the ruin made of our streets. Some of the field
    is missing. Rumour is

the cormorant-minded have deserted. Scholars,
    we've work, apparatus

we must restore, laboratories to right. The aviaries
    want for noise. We've still

gestures of attention, and flocks taking wing,
    have reasons their own.

Animals and Vehicles / Animals and Vehicles

The vestibule's lit by a light nothing cows,
and can't be quenched. A trouble to the monks,
who try to comprehend the trick the synapses
play is to imply everything's advanced
and everything's organic. That the sequence
from vespers to matins matters, that the triumph

is in the bellrope unless the triumph
is outside the foot-thick walls where cows
have a cud and cud and pasture sequence
and watch. They watch outside the cassocked monks
inside stilled by the comfort of light advanced
in the unwindowed places, as though a synapse

between cloistered and beyond is the synapse
of translation and inhabited. The triumph
is transcending the boundary. Yet who advanced
beyond the fields beyond the walls, their cowls
thrown back with the glee and abandon of monks
recognizing the world for what it is, a sequence

limited by observances? Sequence and consequence,
the kingdom is buried in a field of synapses
like a treasure the cows and the monks
are equally likely to find. That, a triumph?
The fold will be found in the field, the cows
cogitate in the scriptorium, the flock's advanced

to the world beyond and found it not advanced,
not in any sense of the word: the same sequence
of events and observances and monks and cows
applies. And the monks are stranded. Their synapses
have taken their Latin hostage. The cows triumph
by taking a lesson from Bede which the monks

delivered to the air outside like foolish monks
trying to pass through windows like the advance
of swallows through halls and as camels triumph
by entering the needle of heaven. The sequence
is always told in sign language: despite synapses
the monks within no more speak than cows

and in the catalogue they pass for cows as monks
for synaptic ascension. How we've advanced
since vespers, a sequence ending in triumph.

The Book of Encouragement & Consolation

—Eva of Wilton

There have been men also, want perpetual
    as hum and underbrush there must have,
        though they call it hermitage. Entrance

to their closeting. Think of darkness a hand
    reaching, the urge to speech prevented (tongue
        composed, the parched throat no longer

a threshold)—all you own of touch is stone
    and wall. If we were ourselves men, if we were
        allowed the nursing of plants without, allowed

without... We are told our solitude is for promise,
    our trappings a spur to wisdom. Men set down
        what our solitude requires, that it removes

the body. Do you dare imagine the anchoress
    laying a hand on her own flesh? Silence lasts
        only to its next breaking.
                If ascetic, we are imperfect.
                If remembered, companied.

Your Multivocalic

The lights

come up. We the cast seated beside you. You

the fault line between colours. Submerged blue
to shale peach or each act happening simultaneously:

the inter-national war, the unending medieval, the tent

an epicenter, an origin. Something inside
hurts like mineral in a vein. Sounds

heard within the tent and cavern the skull is,

the self at its polyphonic best, you were all the time
the next illogical step in the dramatic monologue.

We but ringmastered this. Find ourselves

audienced. Left to towns which branch like alveoli,
as permeable as, as collapsible as. Migrant into

the hope that distance is a solace remaining isn't.

New British

Aboard, at home
again, and now a little wind but little wind
and stone and green. Dead of winter, and
this beech wood's mind next to my own skin.

November: what was it you said again
                    there by the river—

    The King and Queen of Dumfriesshire.
    The Long Man of Wilmington winces.

    The drone of a saw exactly as the setting
    sun jolts on, the houses petered out.

A cairn of rain. The way I learned the year
began with baleful auguries. I loved the rain.
I loved the light, of course, next to my own skin.

II

Herring-bone and fern, my friends hunted
beasts four-fathoms long, but perfectly gentle.

The sea is made of ponds. I'm fond, nereids
and nymphs. I have in my possession
the *Kentish Independent*. Let there be braziers.

        This could be the mind's antechamber.

III

Clara, your house at childhood's end,
    the wind in a field of corn. If I remember,

his first letter: "the first rule is to pacify
    the wives." One day, no one sees me.

  In the sleeping ward, in the centre
  of the sheep-field,   lemurs somehow
  at the lilt of the road. This Roman road.

IV

Brethren, I know that many of you have come here today
  after the full-day's westward drive:

anything can be forgotten. Someone explained once that
  the past is the antithesis of burglary

  V

and you ask whether I am ever coming back.

$[\dots]$

If You Could See the Motorists'
Gloves and Leathers!

Learned to count this world in hands and now in feet and
for long, Saint Brendan. What's to distance but a thinking
through—this flap'll open someone into something else. All
this sense... Once thought, St. Brendan, I'd adventure from
and explore what it was they talk about beyond. Have the
eyes for it. Thought I'd try again a ride or two, a sideshow,
the rolling-coaster, the duck shy. But these aught-to-mobiles
gathered here and such a work to do. To think the things he-
and-she forgot between these cars. What you miss. Appetite,
St. Brendan. Where'd these go, if we found ourselves in one
of them not just attending? What are my eyes for, Father, but
for widening? To the tent's edge, Father?

Notes

The epigraph comes from H.G. Wells' short-story "The Country of the Blind."

"Tonight, there's a lot of fancy cars in the all-purpose magical tent," which begins "If You Could See the Motorists' Gloves and Leathers!" comes from a 2005 Nature Theater of Oklahoma production, *Kasimir und Karoline,* and was voiced by the actor Robert M. Johanson.

"The Anvil That Comes Before Your Civilisation" is for Carey McHugh and is after her poem "The Lynx That Comes Just Before Your Grief."

Monika Otter, the translator of St. Goscelin of Bertin's 11th century *Liber Confortatius* (The Book of Encouragement & Consolation), describes it as "a letter of guidance to a female recluse by her male spiritual advisor." Eva of Wilton, Goscelin's addressee, was sent to become an anchoress in France; Katherine O'Brien O'Keefe's reading of the text suggests that Eva's imprisonment was a punishment for Goscelin's amorous intentions.

Monster Theory is the title of an essay collection edited by Jeffrey Jerome Cohen. His introductory essay, "Monster Culture: Seven Theses," provided the inspiration and several key phrases for "Monster Theory."

"The Ruin is a ruin, yet even beyond this convenient status of its material text, the poem raises the spectre of language as an unhomely dwelling place, as a crafted enclosure host to wine-flushed voices yet subject to decay over time and space," writes Jess R. Fenn in her essay "On The Ruin, the Riddle-poem, and (not) being there."

The question which begins "The Wide Receiver Declares Himself Ready" adapts a proverb attributed to King Alfred.

"Annuls the Space/Time Experience" is for Timothy Donnelly. "The dream of language" is also the title of an essay in Giorgio Agamben's *The End of the Poem: Studies in Poetics.*

The first and last phrases of "Manufacturing Culture" are adapted from Joseph Bizup's *Manufacturing Culture: Vindications of Early Victorian Industry.*

"Kluyver, the starling man, is all right," the Dutch ethologist Nikolaas Tinbergen wrote in *Nature* in 1945, providing news of the ornithologists after World War II. "Cormorant-minded" was his description of an animal psychologist who spent much of the war hiding in trees where Lekkerkerk cormorants nested.

The cento "New British" uses words and phrases from the "Index of First Lines" to *New British Poetry*.

"After the Last Days of the Circus" is for Priscilla Becker and the Migrant Poetry Workshop.

Acknowledgments

Thanks & affection to those who read and cared about these poems and this book, friends and teachers all: I look forward to stealing horses with you. Lasting gratitude to PB, internal west, end of winter; TD, for 1. the abbey & 2. sonic ghosts; Trevor, possibility & comedy; Gordon, drama, monologues, Brecht etc; Kacy, who kept me hopeful; Liam, driving November, I owe a debt; Mothercage and the tour of '73 (remember?); Division United, *loco* enough to keep me in goal, cheers. A greenery of thanks to Carey, for instructions &c, for her poems especially, always before & beyond me: "language includes a treasury of place, winged and expanding" indeed.

Jess, you keep showing me the road continues—suspense—the way life should be— here's to it continuing. This book belongs with you.

To Stephen, recoverer, inventor; to Christina, keenest eye, sharpest ear; to Terrance Hayes (whoa... right back); to all at Nightboat; to Rrryan, who gave this colour: thank you, most deeply and reverently. I couldn't be better embarked.

I'm grateful to all at the following magazines, where some of these poems appeared:

American Letters & Commentary: "Hereafter," "Interior Horticulture Affair"

The Atlantic: "The Wide Receiver Declares Himself Ready"

Bateau: "If You Could See the Motorists' Gloves and Leathers!"

Boston Review: "The Lost Tin Myth"

Colorado Review: "Manual for Weather," "The Tightrope Walker's Childhood"

Denver Quarterly: "News of the Ornithologists"

Greensboro Review: "Circus Memory," "Earliest Known Record of a Carousel Device"

Laurel Review: "Structural for the Tent"

Ninth Letter: "Manufacturing Culture"

Tarpaulin Sky: "Annuls the Space-Time Experience"

Tight: "New British"

Tin House: "The Book of Encouragement and Consolation"

Verse: "Scarecrow Work"

Some poems are forthcoming at the free online audio archive From the Fishouse, www.fishouse.org. My gratitude to them for their support.

Thank you to Monica Youn, who selected some of these poems for the Bennett Prize from the Academy of American Poets.

Some of these poems appeared in a chapbook, *Monster Theory* (P.S.A. 2008), selected by Kevin Young for a New York Chapbook Fellowship. My thanks to him for his encouragement, and to all at the Poetry Society of America.

After the Last Days of the Circus

to awning and entrance
you [...] welcome

repurposed vintage devices.

A fixstitch
in vestments,
manufacts.

Torn   gloves, recycling
a globe turning us

toward horizon, applause.

Redstriped, whitestriped,
unrolling, staging a site,
a plausible circuit,
, sure habits.

This threshold of without,
this collapse now here
remains. Remembrances.
The adventure from this

into canvas
to awning and entrance

ABOUT NIGHTBOAT BOOKS

Nightboat Books, a nonprofit organization, seeks to develop audiences for writers whose work resists convention and transcends boundaries. We publish books rich with poignancy, intelligence, and risk. Please visit our website, www.nightboat.org, to learn more about us and how you can support our future publications.

NIGHTBOAT TITLES IN PRINT

The Lives of a Spirit/Glasstown: Where Something Got Broken by Fanny Howe
The Truant Lover by Juliet Patterson (Winner of the 2004 Nightboat Poetry Prize)
Radical Love: 5 Novels by Fanny Howe
Glean by Joshua Kryah (Winner of the 2005 Nightboat Poetry Prize)
The Sorrow and the Fast of It by Nathanaël (Nathalie Stephens)
Envelope of Night: Selected and Uncollected Poems, 1966-1990 by Michael Burkard
In the Mode of Disappearance by Jonathan Weinert
        (Winner of the 2006 Nightboat Poetry Prize)
Your Body Figured by Douglas A. Martin
Dura by Myung Mi Kim
Absence Where As (Claude Cahun and the Unopened Book) by Nathanaël (Nathalie Stephens)

FORTHCOMING TITLES

Tiresias: The Collected Poems of Leland Hickman
Century of Clouds by Bruce Boone
Poetic Intention by Édouard Glissant

Our books are available through Small Press Distribution (www.spdbooks.org).

The following indviduals have supported the publication of this book. We thank them for their generosity and commitment to the mission of Nightboat Books:

Anonymous	J. Carey and Nancy McHugh
Jericho Brown	Sean C. Stafford
Katherine Dimma	Benjamin Taylor
Sarah Heller	Loyal and Margie Tingley
Loop Dance Company/LoopEd	

In addition, this book has been made possible, in part, by a grant from the New York State Council on the Arts Literature Program.

State of the Arts

NYSCA

green press
I N I T I A T I V E

Nightboat Books is committed to preserving ancient forests and natural resources. We elected to print this title on 30% postconsumer recycled paper, processed chlorine-free. As a result, for this printing, we have saved:

1 Trees (40' tall and 6-8" diameter)
440 Gallons of Wastewater
1 million BTUs of Total Energy
56 Pounds of Solid Waste
106 Pounds of Greenhouse Gases

Nightboat Books made this paper choice because our printer, Thomson-Shore, Inc., is a member of Green Press Initiative, a nonprofit program dedicated to supporting authors, publishers, and suppliers in their efforts to reduce their use of fiber obtained from endangered forests.

For more information, visit www.greenpressinitiative.org

Environmental impact estimates were made using the Environmental Defense Paper Calculator. For more information visit: www.edf.org/papercalculator